CONTENT

Phonics

Grades K - 1

Designed to reinforce essential skills!

By completing this phonics workbook, your child will gain systematic practice in the following concepts:

- Identifying Short Vowels
- Identifying Long Vowels
- Reading Colour Words
- Identifying Initial and Final Letter Sounds

Colour in this picture.

Print and read the colours.

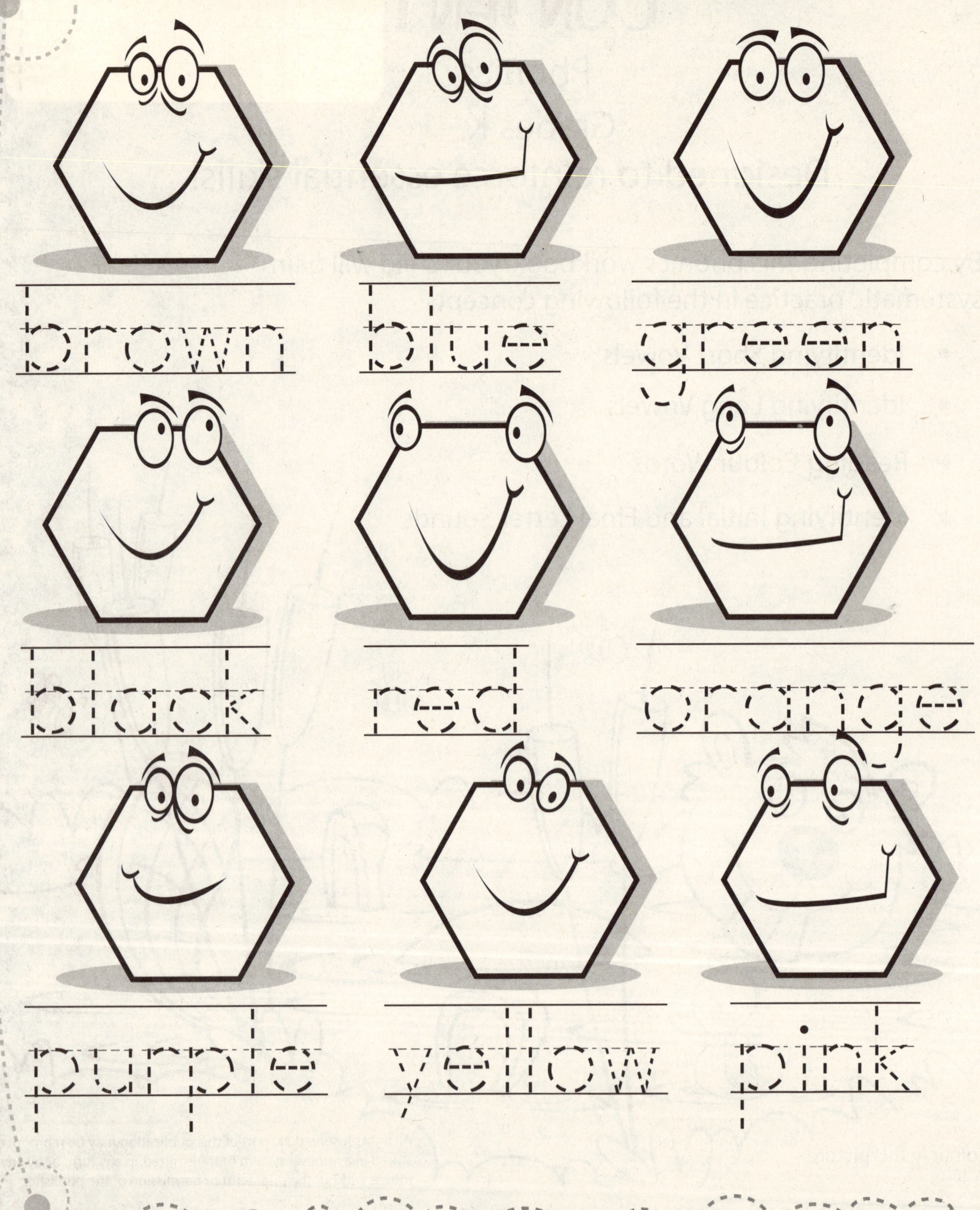

Short a

Cat has the sound of short **a**.
Say the name of each picture.
Colour **ONLY** the pictures that have a short **a** sound.
Trace and read the words that have a short **a** sound.

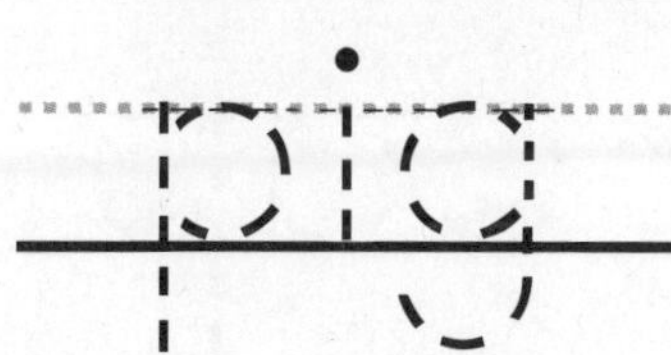

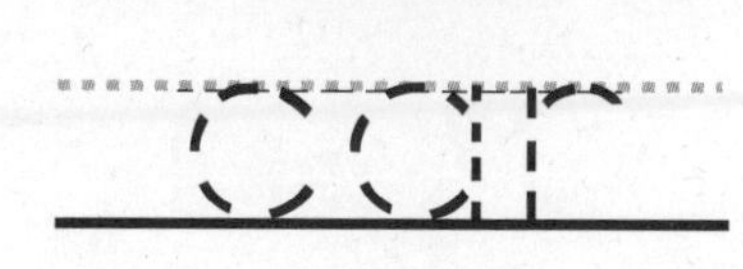

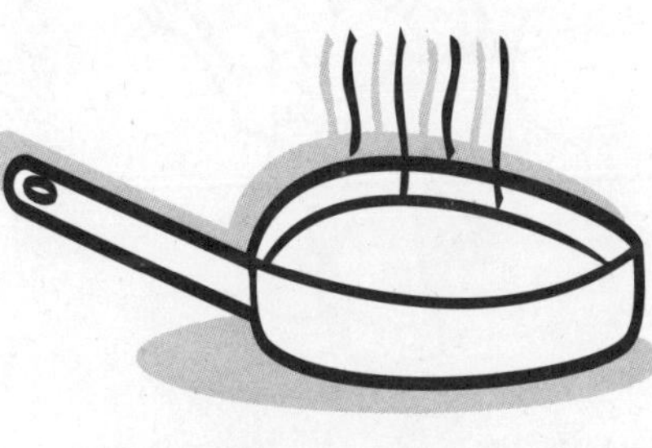

Print two other words that have a short **a** sound.

Short a

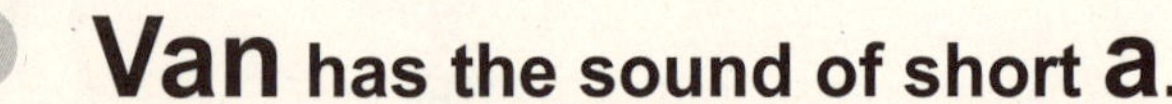

Van has the sound of short **a**.

Say the name of each picture.

Colour ONLY the pictures that have a short a sound.

Trace and read the words that have a short a sound.

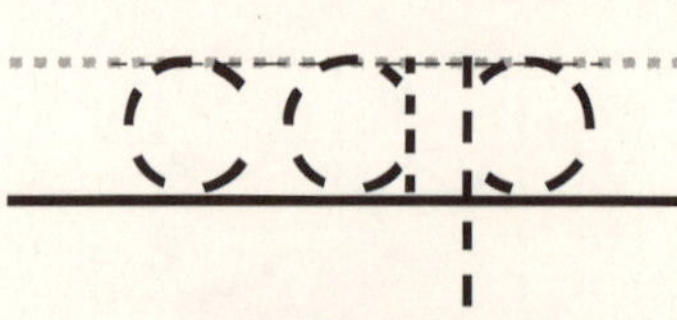

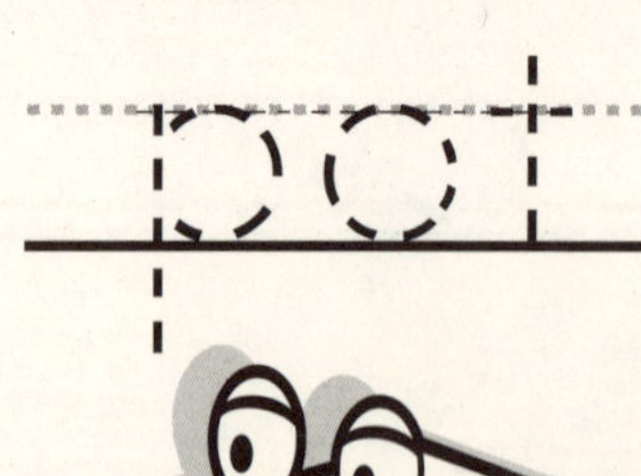

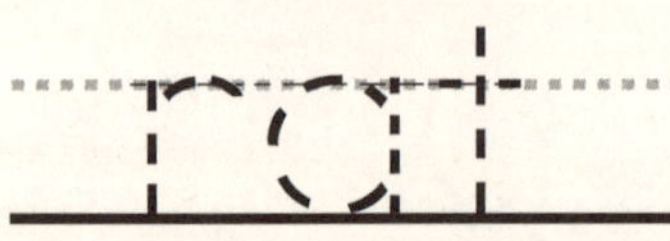

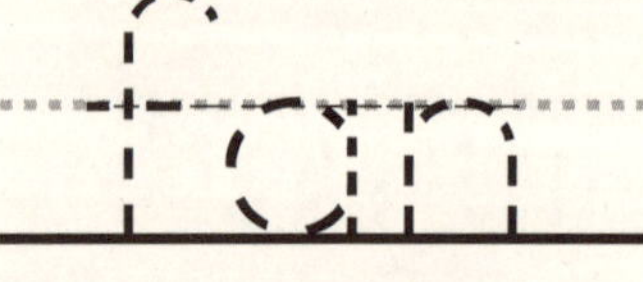

box

Print two other words that have a short a sound.

Short a

Match the correct word to each picture.

Practice reading each word.

bat

pan

cap

van

mat

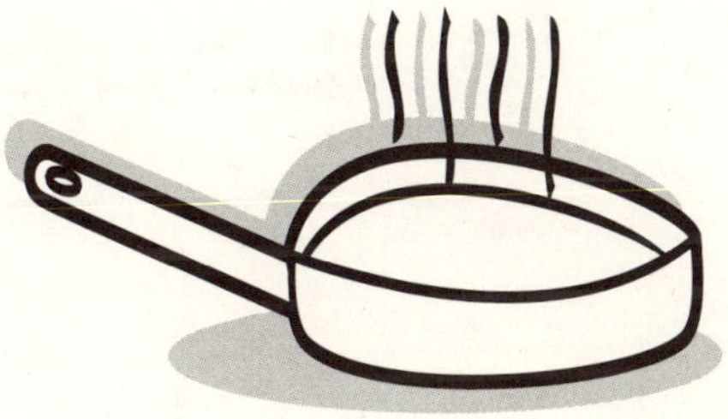

rat

Short i

Bib has the sound of short **i**.

Say the name of each picture.

Colour **ONLY** the pictures that have a short **i** sound.

Trace and read the words that have a short **i** sound.

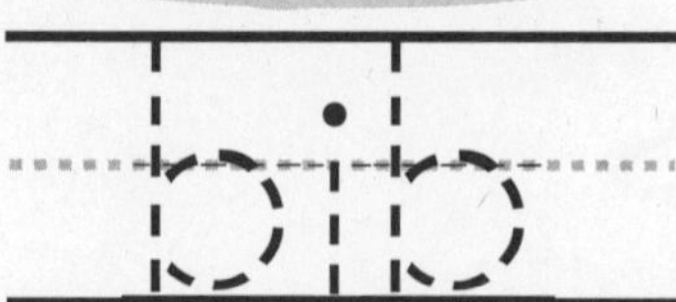

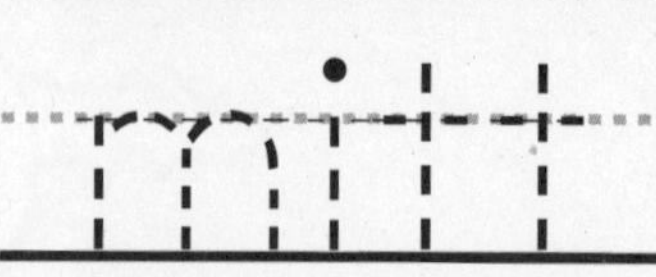

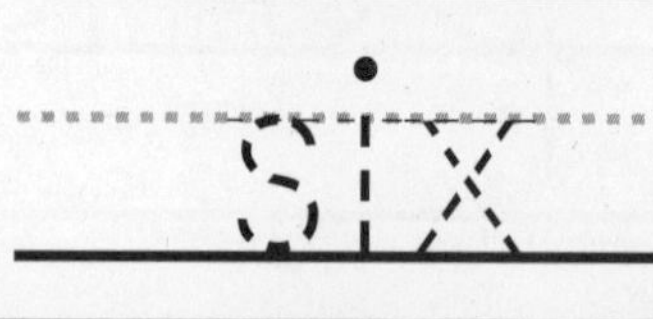

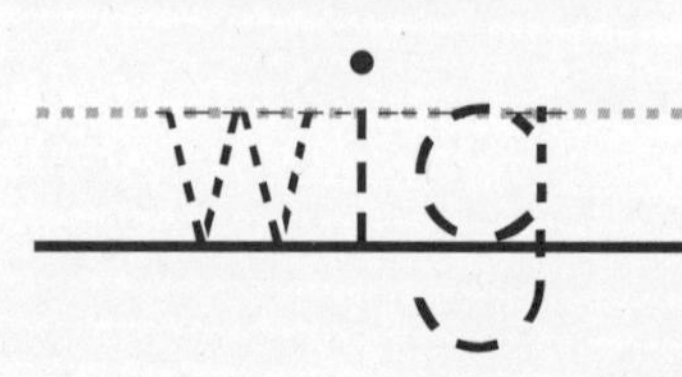

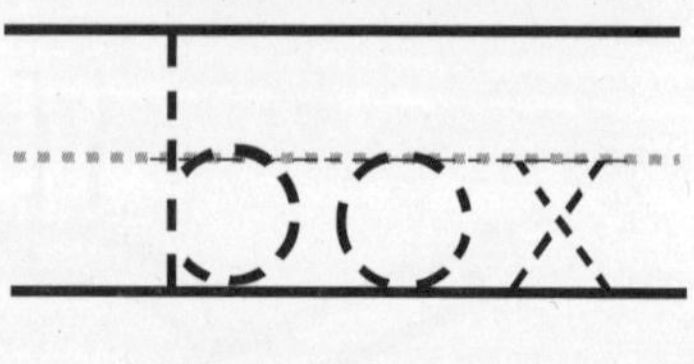

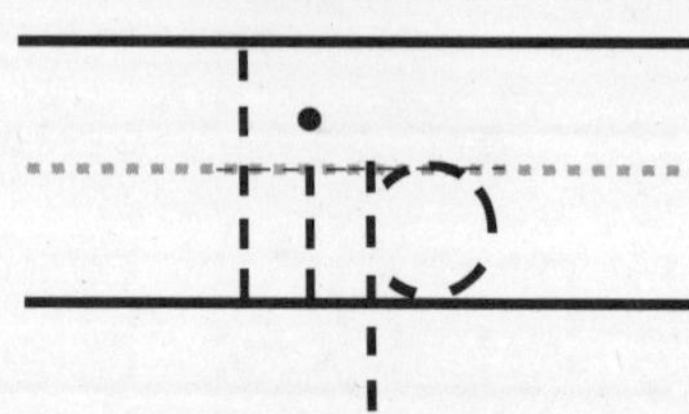

Print two other words that have a short **i** sound.

Short i

Hill has the sound of short **i**.
Say the name of each picture.
Colour ONLY the pictures that have a short i sound.
Trace and read the words that have a short i sound.

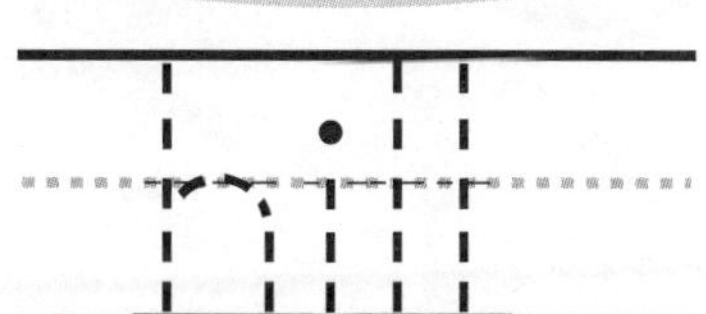

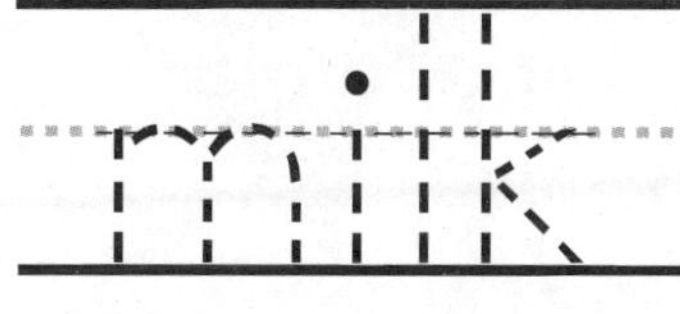

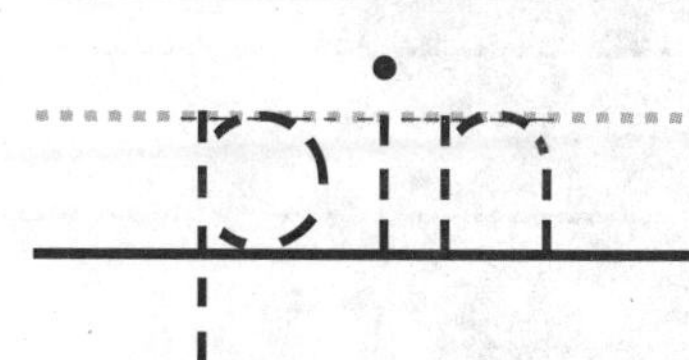

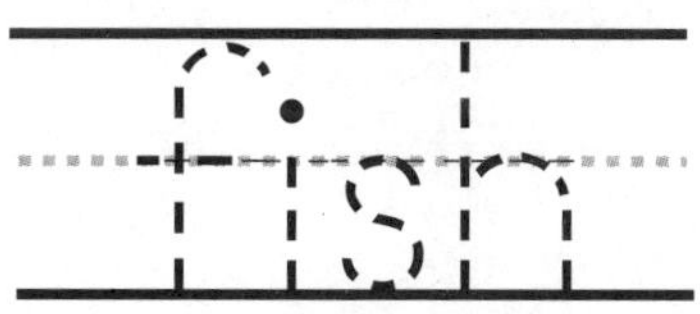

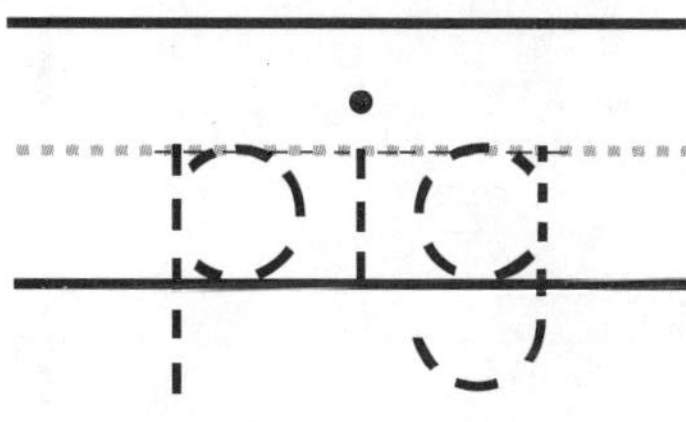

Print two other words that have a short i sound.

Short i

Match the correct word to each picture.
Practice reading each word.

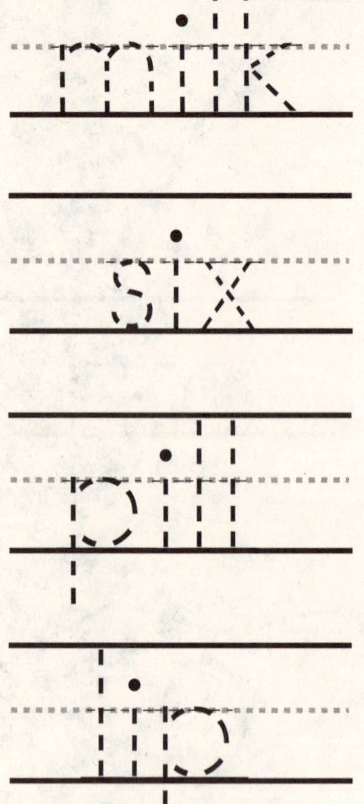

Short e

Jet has the sound of short **e**.
Say the name of each picture.
Colour ONLY the pictures that have a short e sound.
Trace and read the words that have a short e sound.

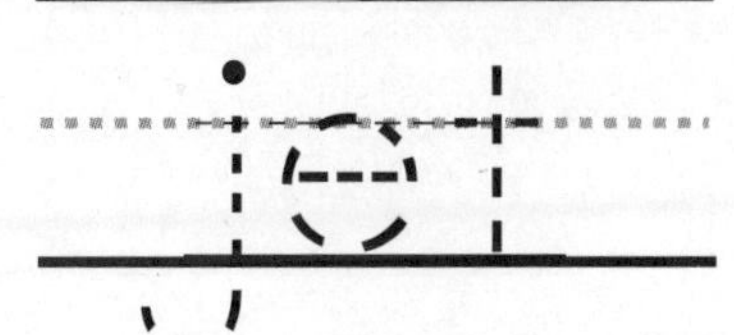

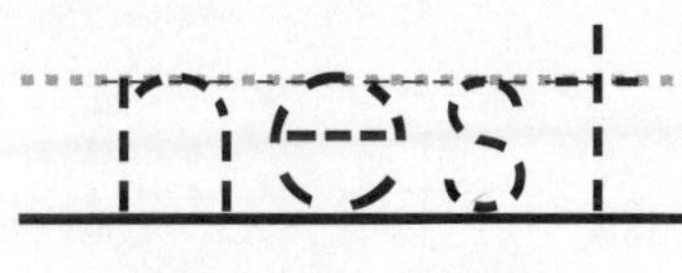

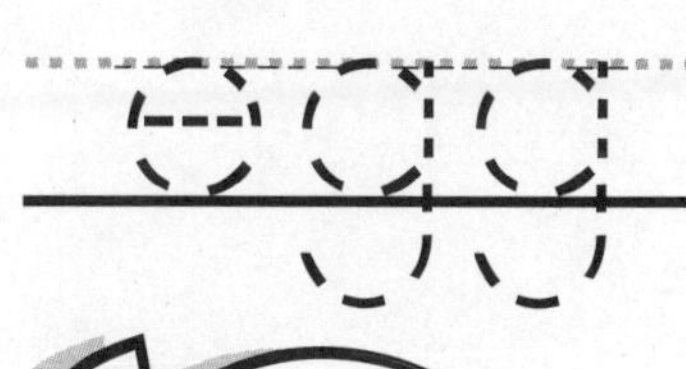

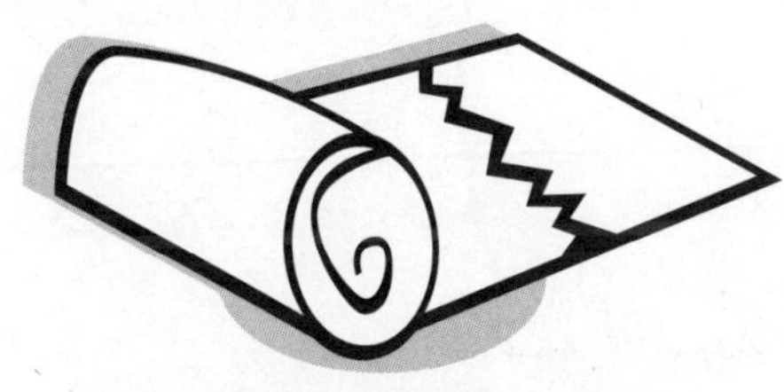

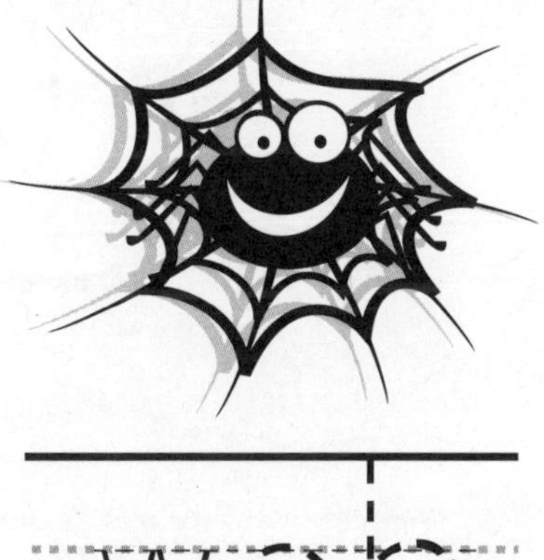

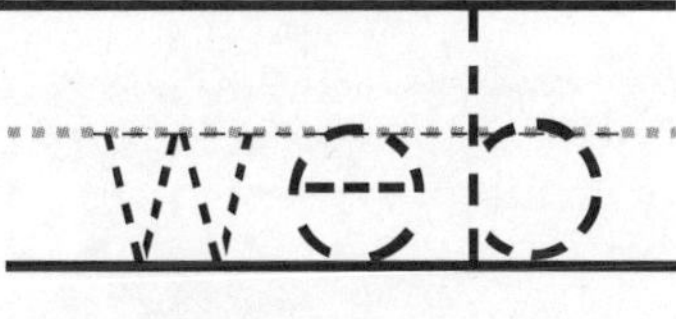

pig

Print two other words that have a short e sound.

Short e

Net has the sound of short **e**.
Say the name of each picture.
Colour **ONLY** the pictures that have a short **e** sound.
Trace and read the words that have a short **e** sound.

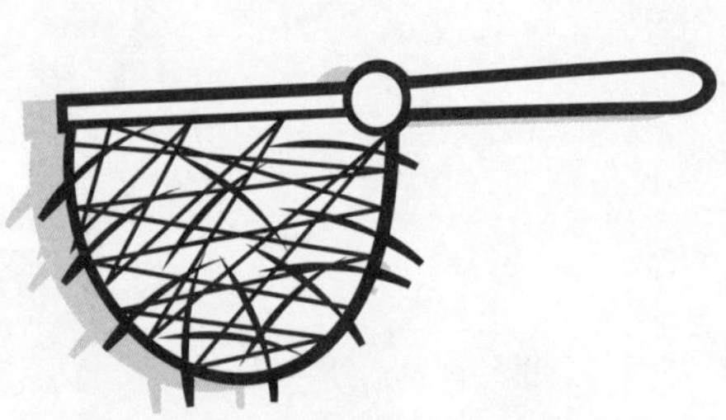

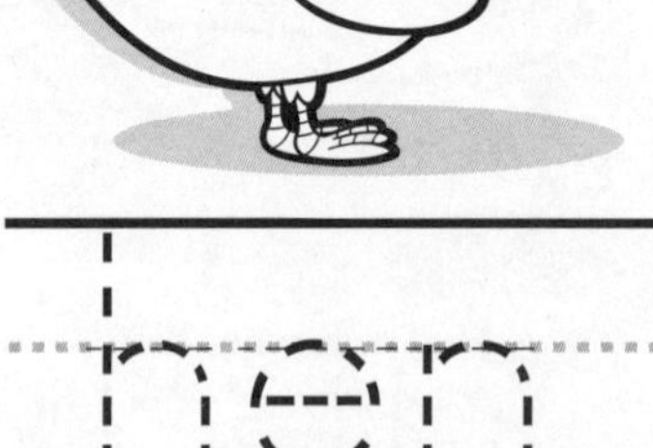

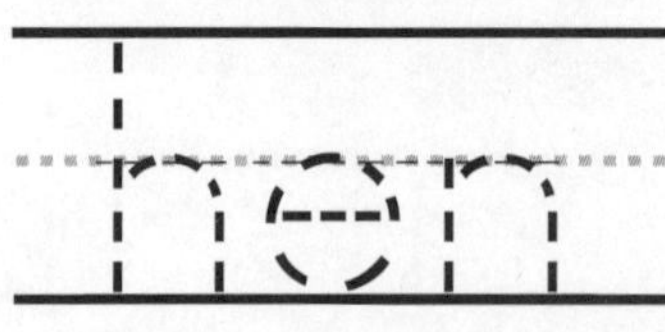

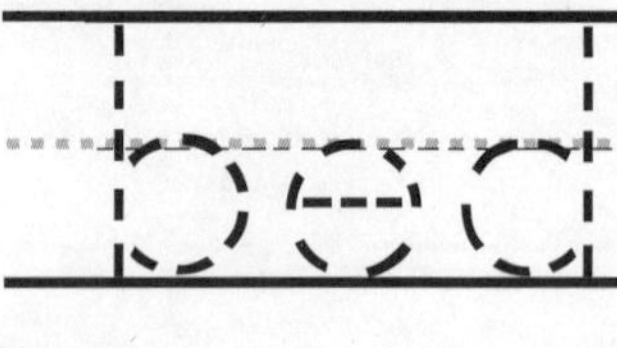

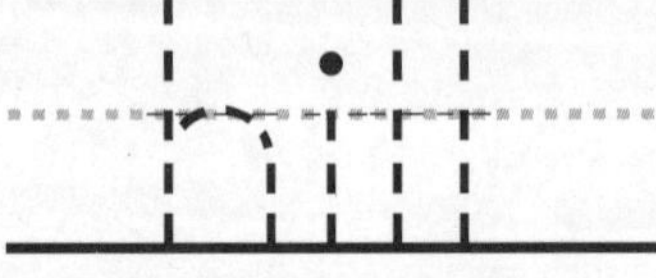

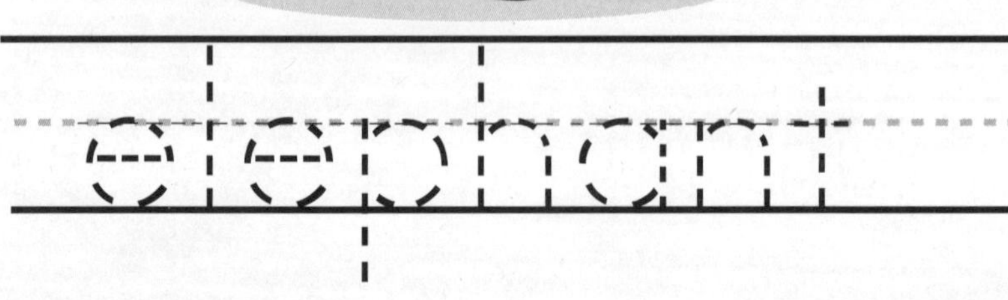

Print two other words that have a short **e** sound.

Short e

Match the correct word to each picture.
Practice reading each word.

hen

web

jet

nest

egg

bed

Short o

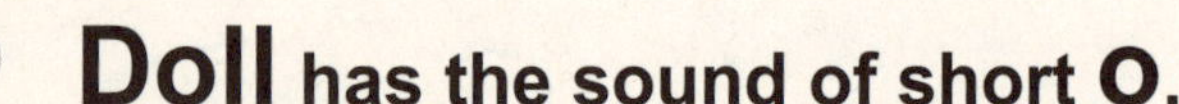

Doll has the sound of short **o**.

Say the name of each picture.

Colour **ONLY** the pictures that have a short **o** sound.

Trace and read the words that have a short **o** sound.

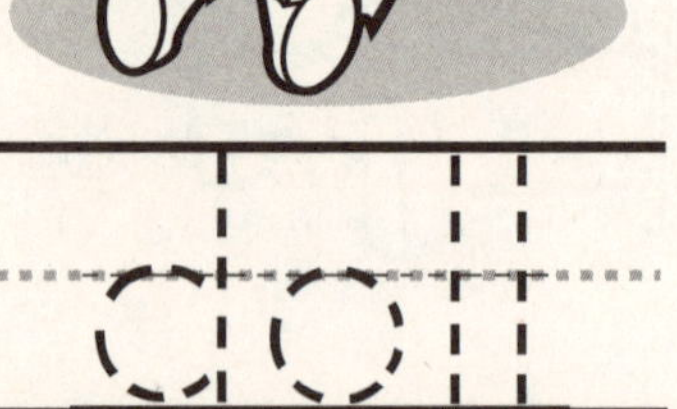

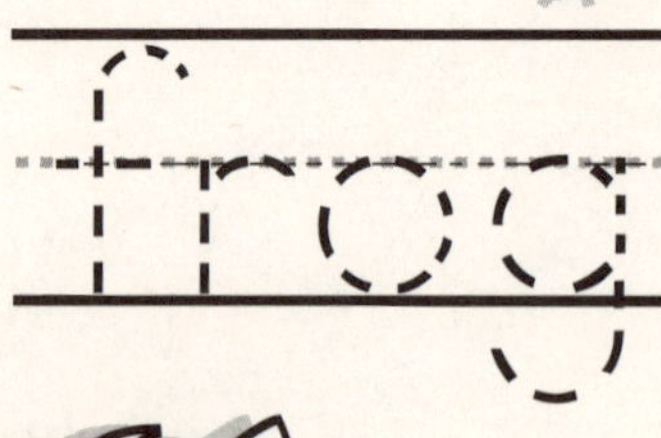

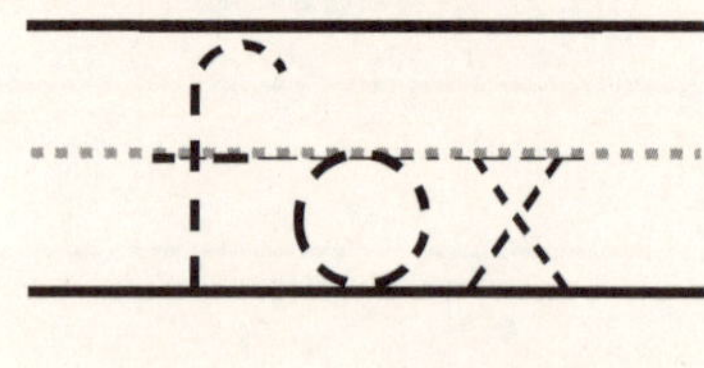

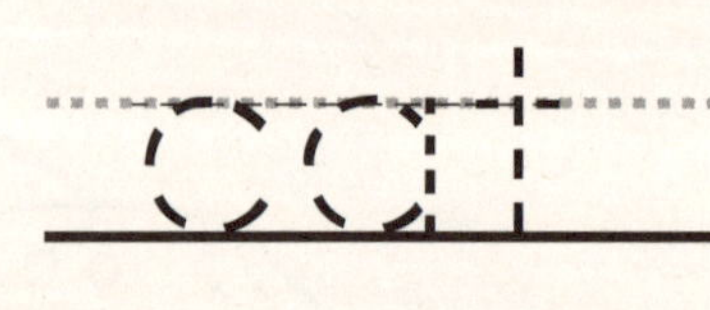

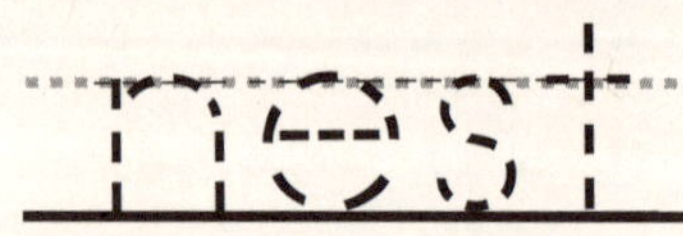

Print two other words that have a short **o** sound.

Short o

Dog has the sound of short **O**.
Say the name of each picture.
Colour **ONLY** the pictures that have a short **O** sound.
Trace and read the words that have a short **O** sound.

dog

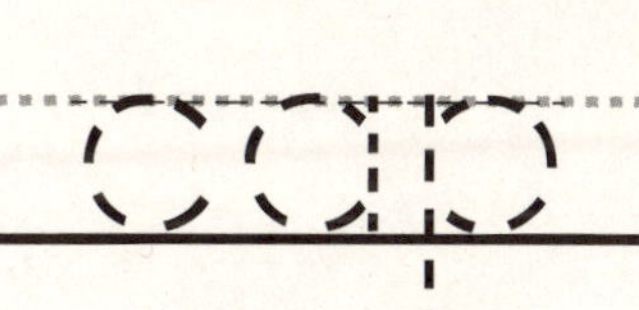

cap

rock

mop

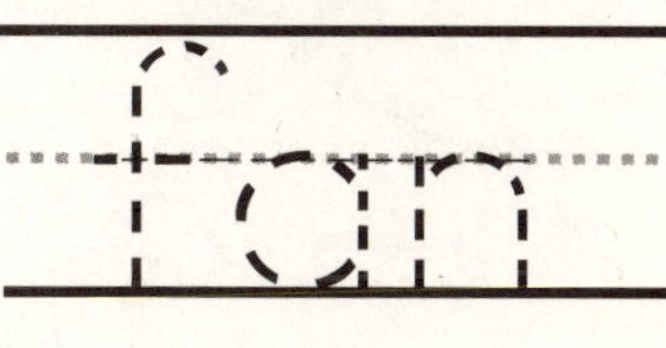

fan

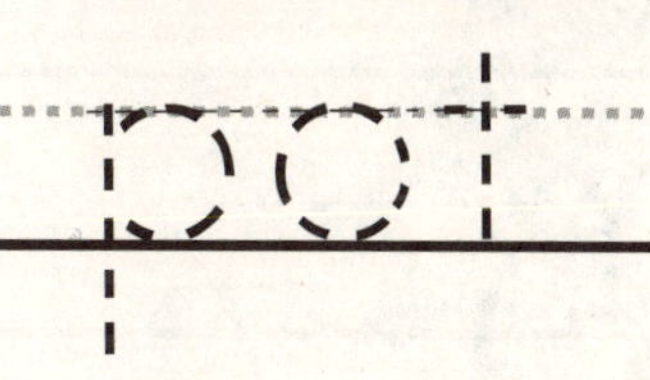

pot

Print two other words that have a short **O** sound.

Short o

Match the correct word to each picture.

Practice reading each word.

Short u

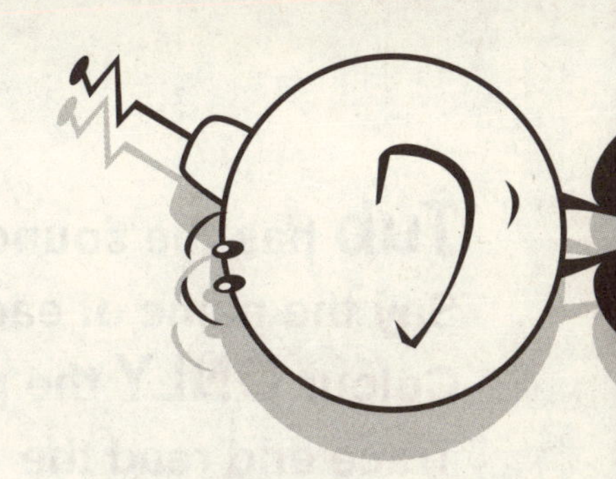

Nut has the sound of short **u**.
Say the name of each picture.
Colour ONLY the pictures that have a short u sound.
Trace and read the words that have a short u sound.

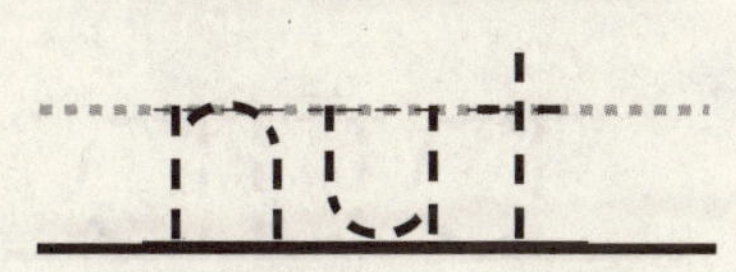

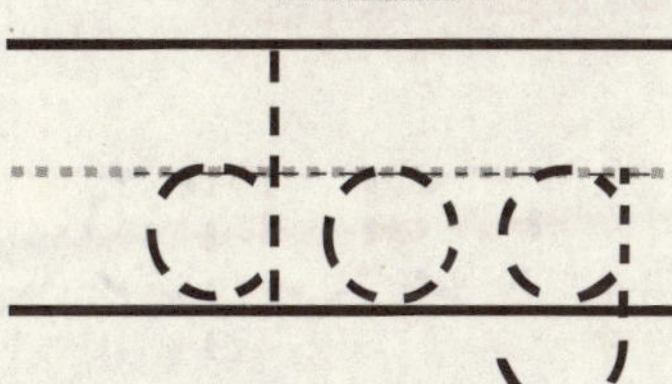

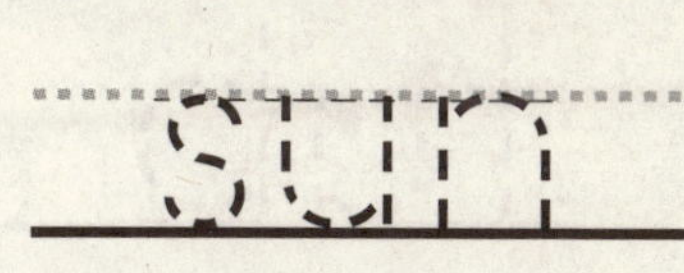

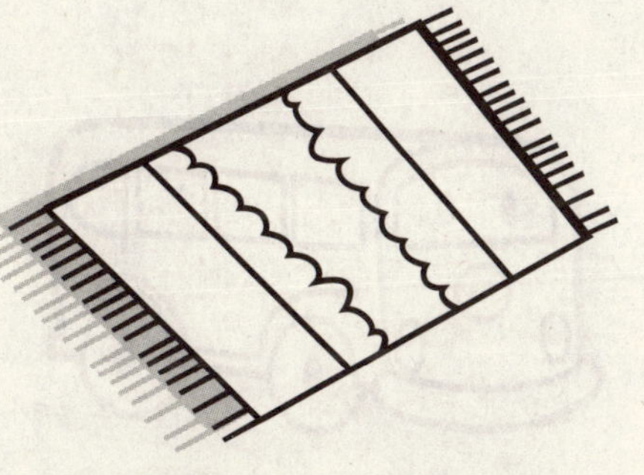

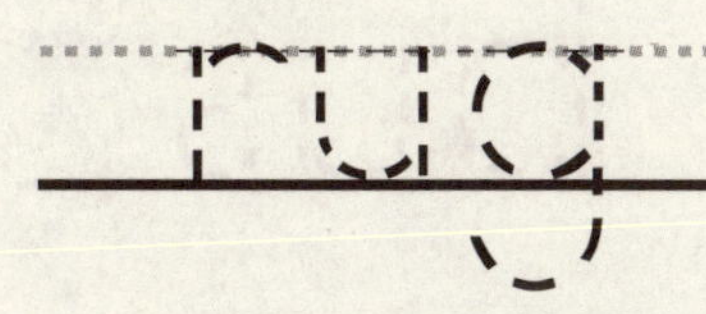

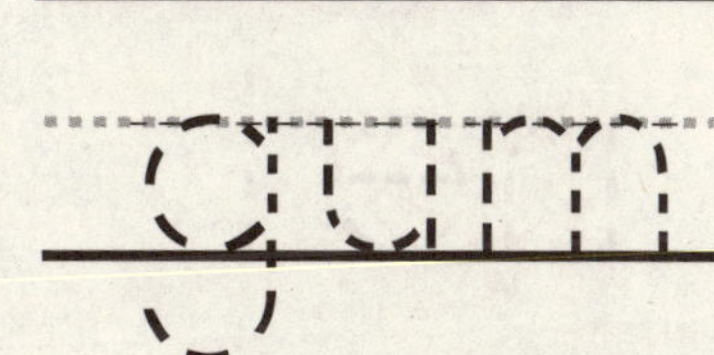

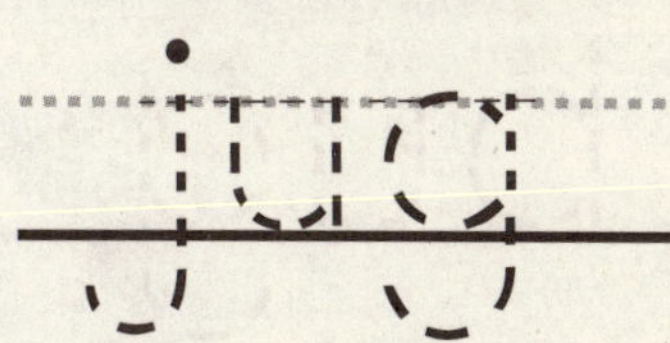

Print two other words that have a short u sound.

Short u

Tub has the sound of short **u**.

Say the name of each picture.

Colour ONLY the pictures that have a short u sound.

Trace and read the words that have a short u sound.

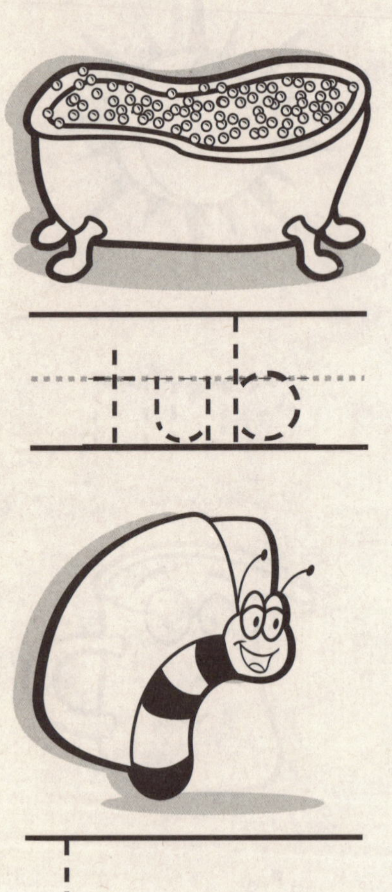

tub

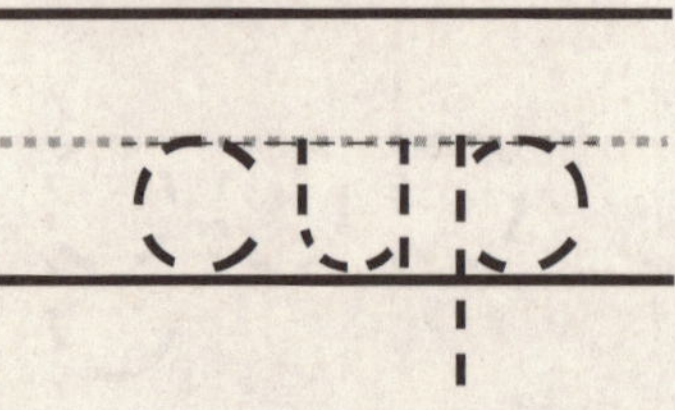

cup

pup

bug

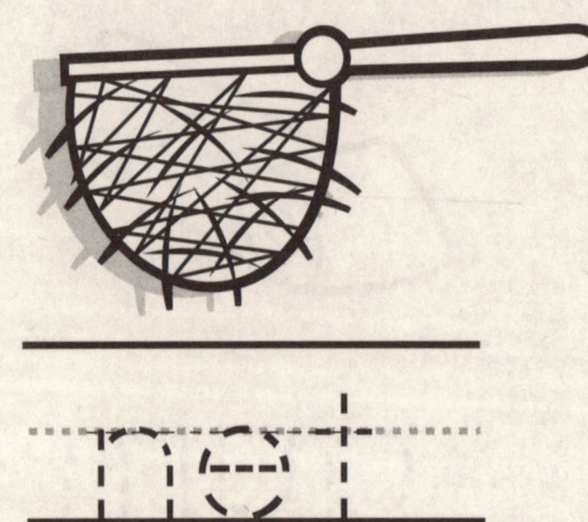

net

bus

Print two other words that have a short u sound.

Short u

Match the correct word to each picture.

Practice reading each word.

bug

bus

pup

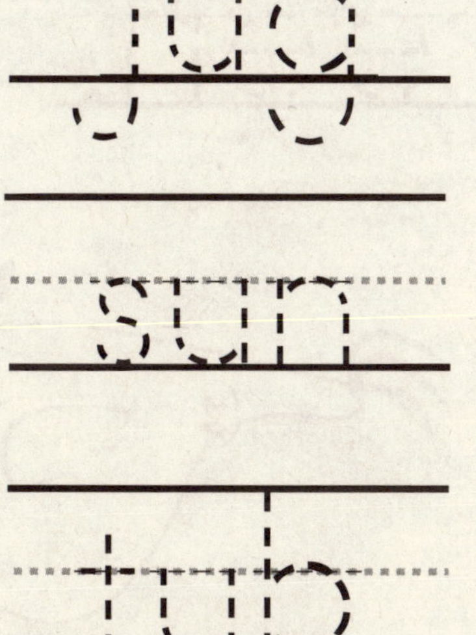

jug

sun

tub

Read and Colour

- Trace and read each sentence.
- Colour each picture.

Read and Colour

Trace and read each sentence.

Colour each picture.

The cup is purple.

The fish is blue.

Read and Colour

Trace and read each sentence.

Colour each picture.

Read and Colour

Trace and read each sentence.

Colour each picture.

Read and Colour

Use the colour key to colour the picture.

Colour the words with a short **a** sound **brown**.

Colour the words with a short **e** sound **red**.

Colour the words with a short **i** sound **pink**.

Colour the words with a short **o** sound **blue**.

Colour the words with a short **u** sound **yellow**.

Read and Colour

Use the colour key to colour the picture.

Colour the words with a short **a** sound ___red___ .

Colour the words with a short **e** sound ___blue___ .

Colour the words with a short **i** sound ___yellow___ .

Colour the words with a short **o** sound ___green___ .

Colour the words with a short **u** sound ___pink___ .

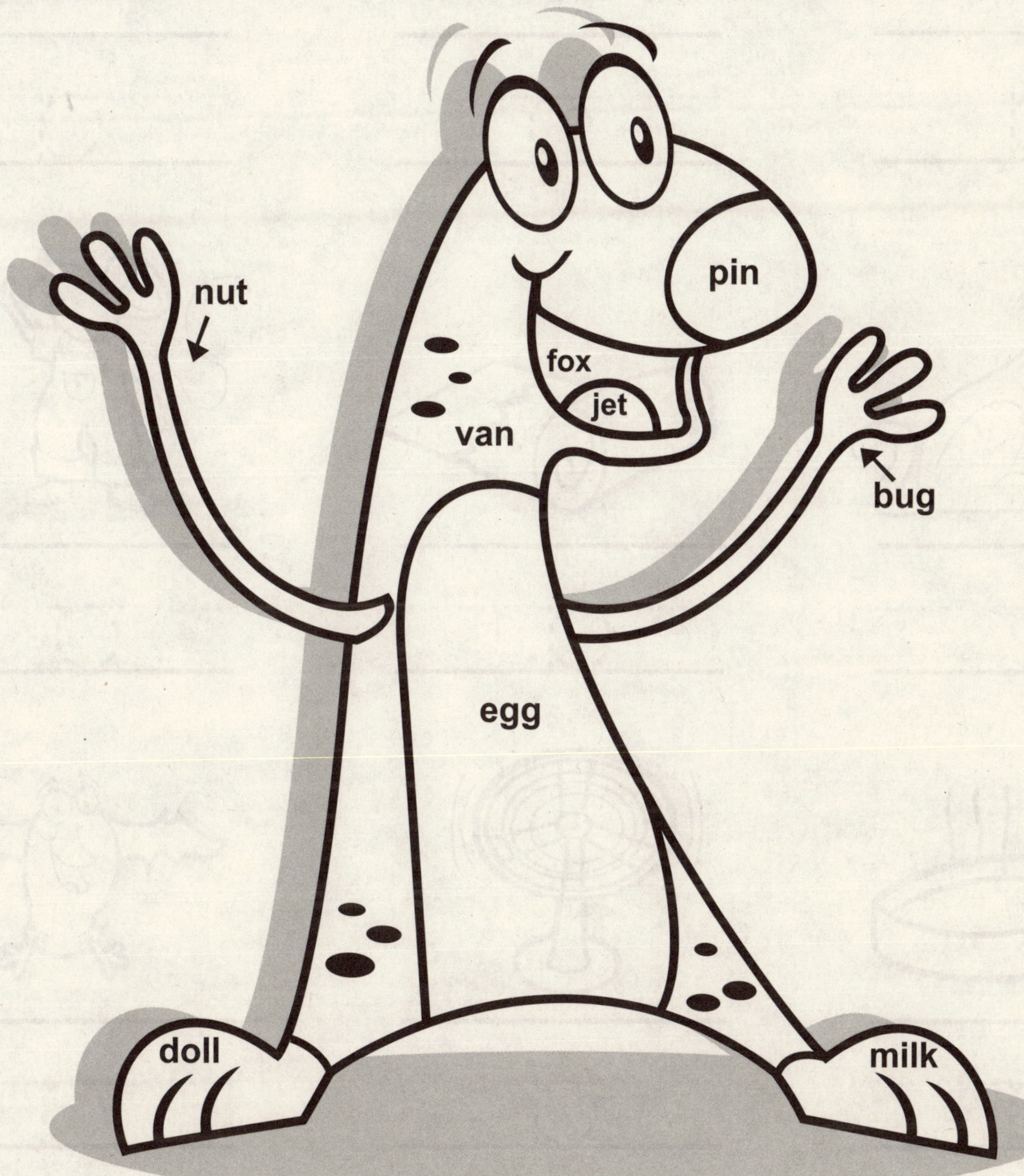

Beginning and Ending Sounds

Say the name of each picture.
Print the letters for its beginning and ending sounds.
Practice reading each word.

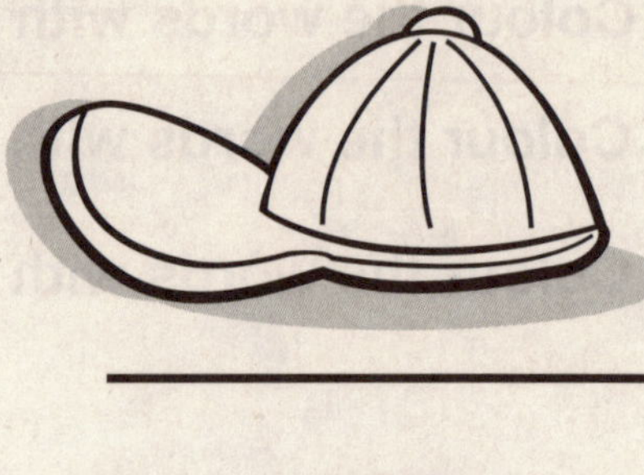

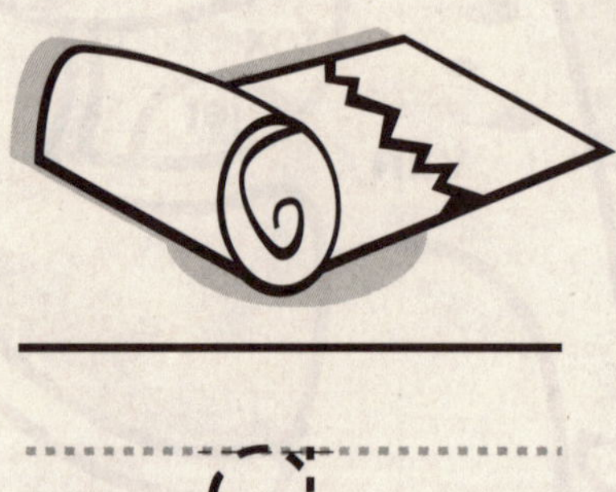

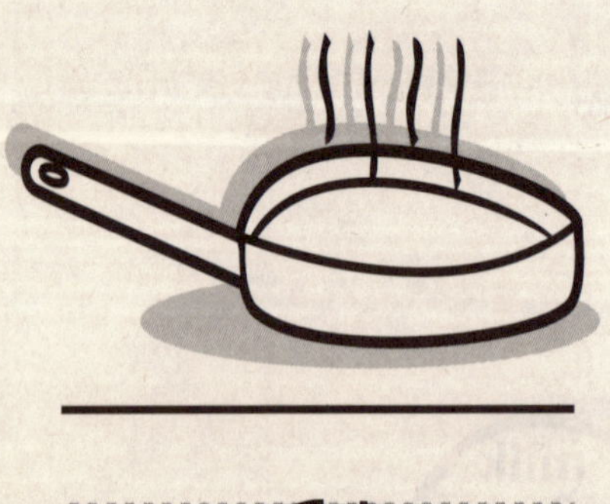

Beginning and Ending Sounds

Say the name of each picture.
Print the letters for its beginning and ending sounds.
Practice reading each word.

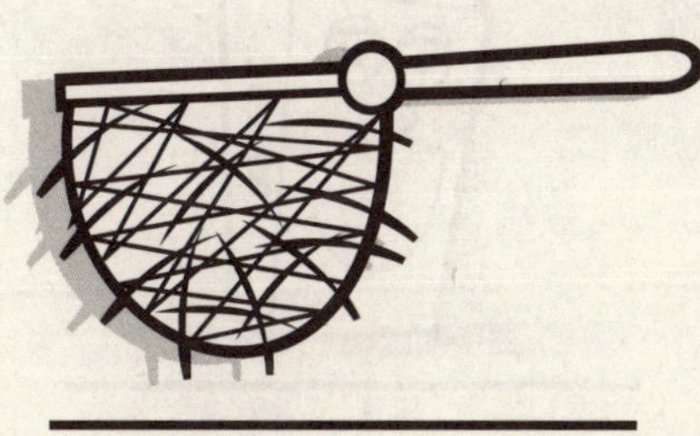

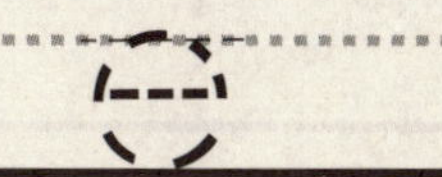

Beginning and Ending Sounds

Say the name of each picture.
Print the letters for its beginning and ending sounds.
Practice reading each word.

Beginning and Ending Sounds

Say the name of each picture.
Print the letters for its beginning and ending sounds.
Practice reading each word.

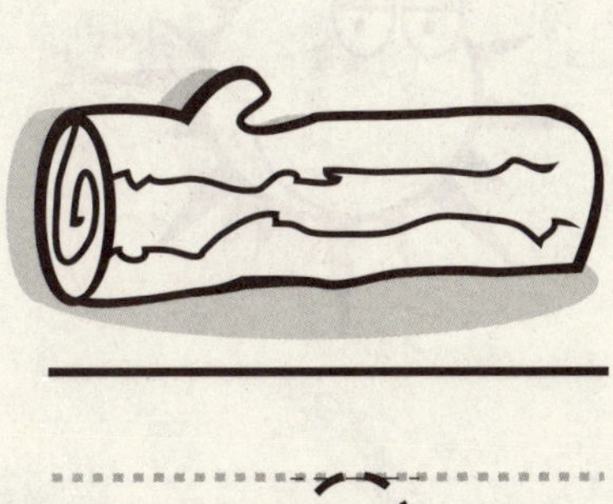

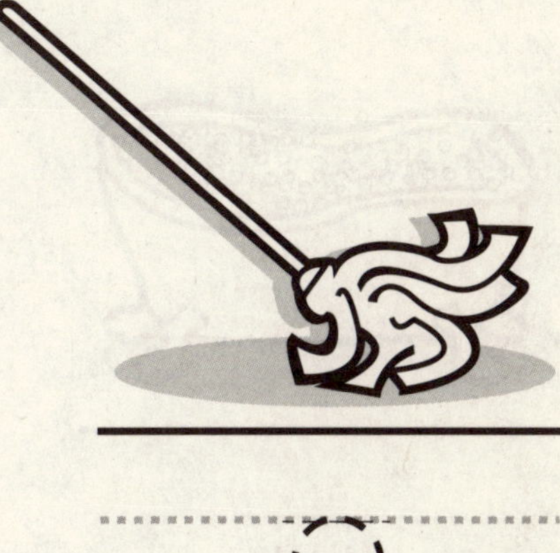

Beginning and Ending Sounds

Say the name of each picture.
Print the letters for its beginning and ending sounds.
Practice reading each word.

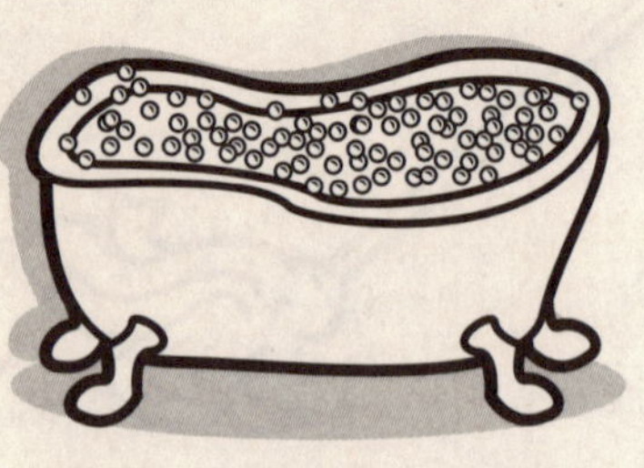

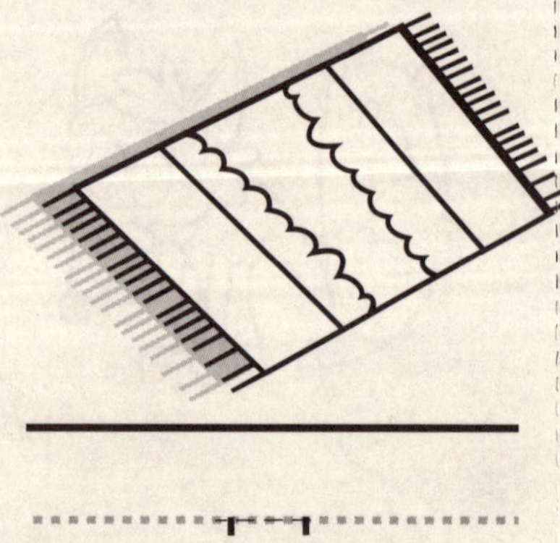

Beginning and Ending Sounds

Say the name of each picture.
Print the letters for its beginning and ending sounds.
Practice reading each word.

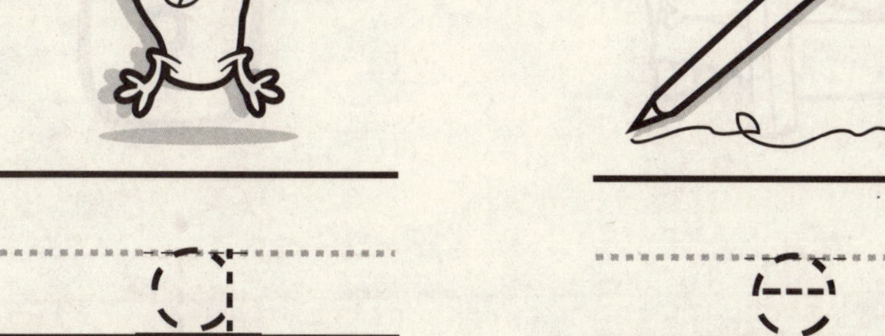

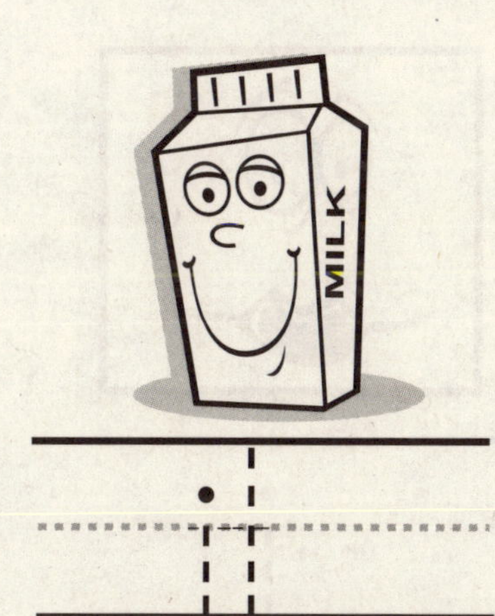

Beginning and Ending Sounds

Say the name of each picture.
Print the letters for its beginning and ending sounds.
Practice reading each word.

u

e

i

a

u

e

i

i

Long a

These words have the long sound of **a**.
Say the name of each picture.
Trace the words.

When there is an **e** at the end of a word, it makes the vowel say it's name.

rake

cane

vase

tape

Colour me!

Print two other words that have a long vowel **a** sound.

Long a

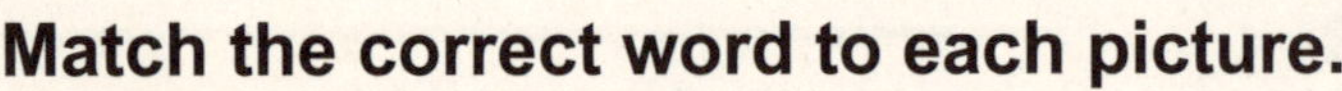

Match the correct word to each picture.

Practice reading each word.

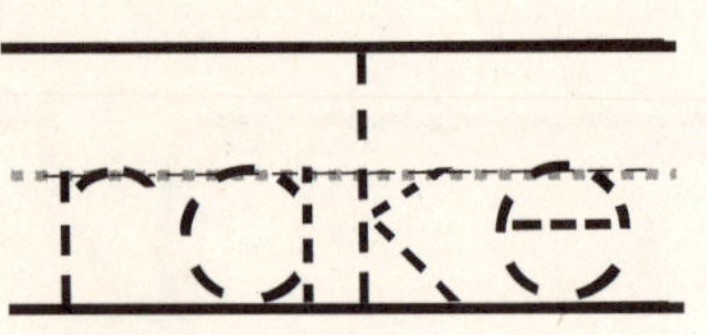

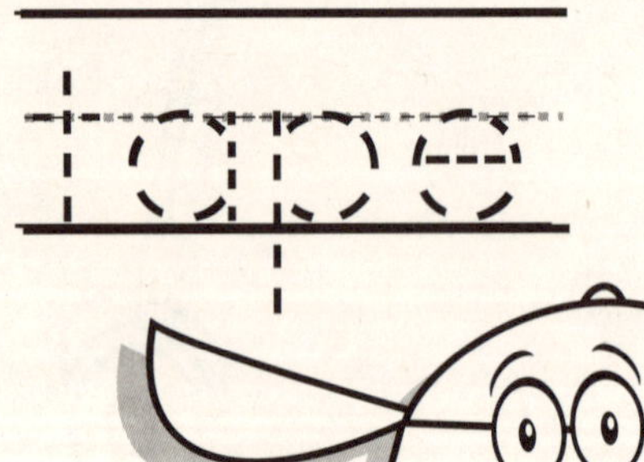

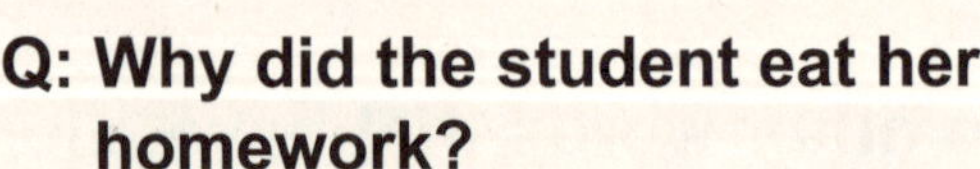

Q: Why did the student eat her homework?
A: Because her teacher said it was a piece of cake!

Long i

These words have the long sound of **i**.
Say the name of each picture.
Trace the words.

Print two other words that have a long vowel **i** sound.

Long i

Match the correct word to each picture.

Practice reading each word.

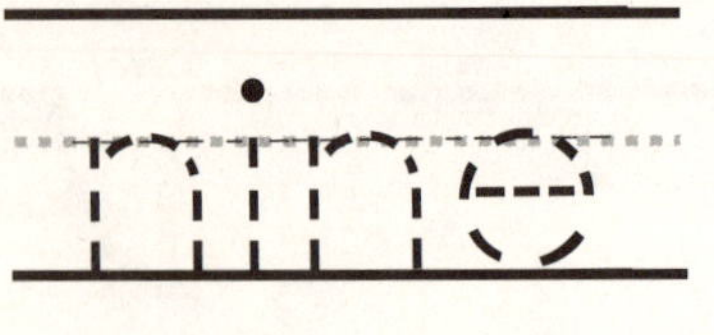

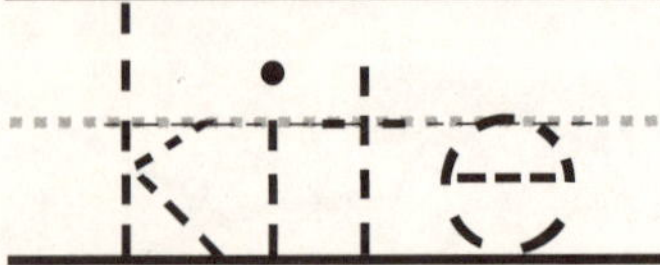

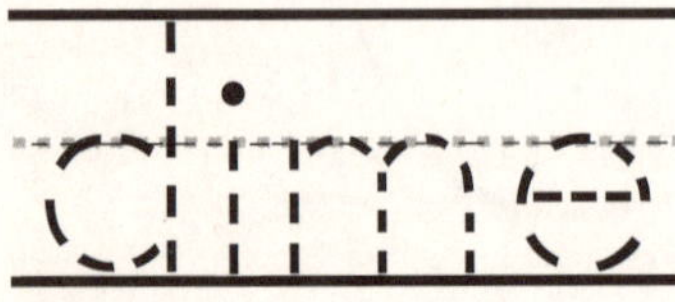

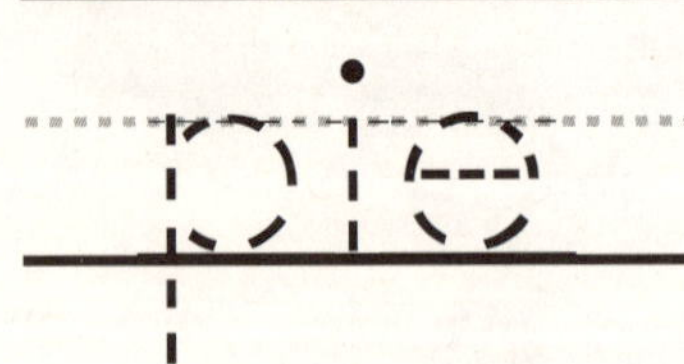

Q: Why did the cow say "baa"?

A: It was learning a new language!

Long o

These words have the long sound of **O**.
Say the name of each picture.
Trace the words.

When there is an **e** at the end of a word, it makes the vowel say it's name.

nose

bone

rose

hose

Colour me!

Print two other words that have a long vowel **O** sound.

Long o

Match the correct word to each picture.

Practice reading each word.

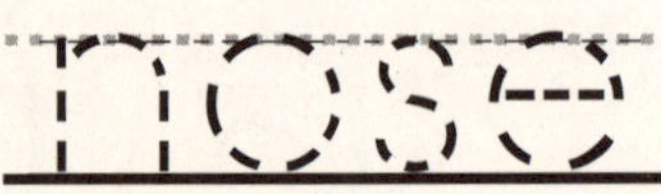

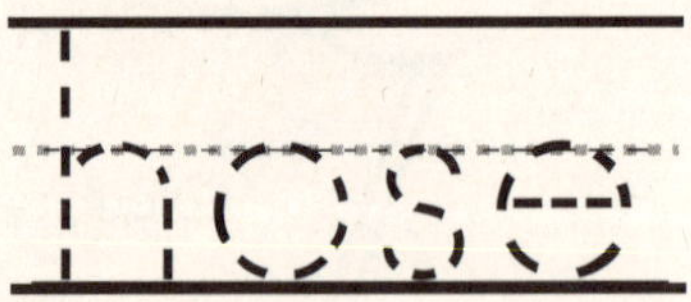

Q: What kind of dog can tell time?

A: A watch dog!

Long u

These words have the long sound of **u**.

Say the name of each picture.

Trace the words.

When there is an **e** at the end of a word, it makes the vowel say it's name.

tube

cube

flute

tune

Colour me!

Print two other words that have a long vowel **u** sound.

Long u

Match the correct word to each picture.

Practice reading each word.

Long e

These words have the long sound of **e**.
Say the name of each picture.
Trace the words.

When there is an **e** at the end of a word, it makes the vowel say it's name.

eel

bee

leaf

tree

Colour me!

Print two other words that have a long vowel **e** sound.

Long e

Match the correct word to each picture.

Practice reading each word.

Read and Colour

Trace and read each sentence.

Colour each picture.

Read and Colour

Trace and read each sentence.

Colour each picture.

The kite is purple.

The pie is blue.

Read and Colour

Trace and read each sentence.

Colour each picture.

The rose is red.

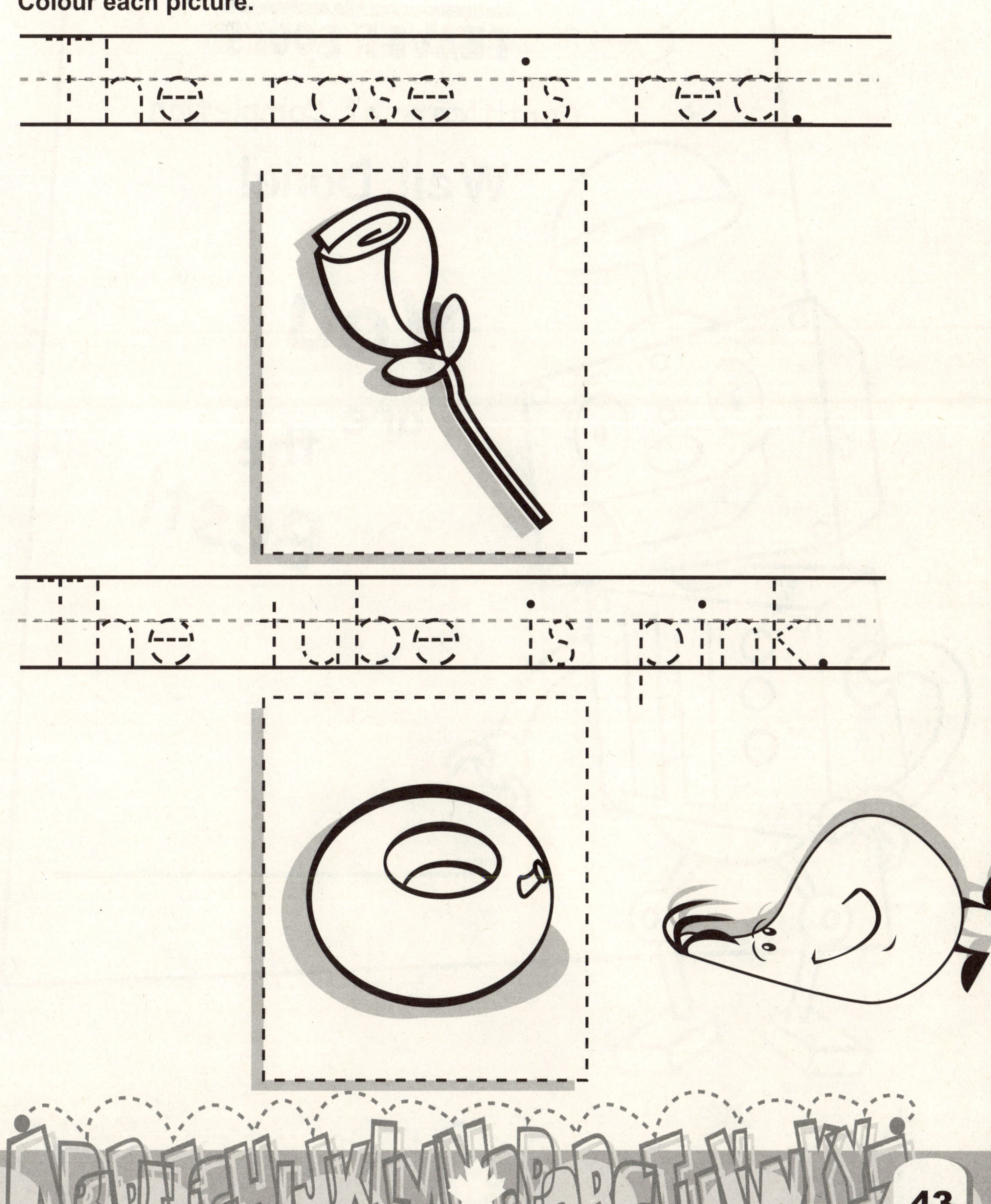

The tube is pink.

BEAVER BOOKS
Certificate of Completion.
Well Done!
You
are the
Best!
Name: